Strength to Flourish

A 52-WEEK GUIDED DEVOTIONAL AND PRAYER JOURNAL

MINISTRY OF SEED AND SOIL

© Copyright 2025 - All rights reserved.

The content contained within this book may not be reproduced, duplicated or transmitted without direct written permission from the author or the publisher.

Under no circumstances will any blame or legal responsibility be held against the publisher, or author, for any damages, reparation, or monetary loss due to the information contained within this book, either directly or indirectly.

Legal Notice:

This book is copyright protected. It is only for personal use. You cannot amend, distribute, sell, use, quote or paraphrase any part, or the content within this book, without the consent of the author or publisher.

Disclaimer Notice:

Please note the information contained within this document is for educational and entertainment purposes only. All effort has been executed to present accurate, up to date, reliable, complete information. No warranties of any kind are declared or implied. Readers acknowledge that the author is not engaged in the rendering of legal, financial, medical or professional advice. The content within this book has been derived from various sources. Please consult a licensed professional before attempting any techniques outlined in this book.

By reading this document, the reader agrees that under no circumstances is the author responsible for any losses, direct or indirect, that are incurred as a result of the use of the information contained within this document, including, but not limited to, errors, omissions, or inaccuracies.

CONTENTS

Introduction 6

EMBRACE NEW BEGINNINGS

Week 1: He Is Making a Way for You 10
Week 2: Reach Forward to Those Things Ahead 12
Week 3: God Works All Things for Good 14
Week 4: Fruitful Even During Affliction 16

RESET YOUR HEART

Week 5: Healing Comes as You Forgive 20
Week 6: Casting Light on Our Shadows 22
Week 7: Creating a New Heart 24
Week 8: A Fully Devoted Heart 26

SECURE YOUR GATES

Week 9: Healing Our Blind Spots 30
Week 10: Restoring Our Spiritual Hearing 32
Week 11: The Power of Our Words 34
Week 12: Transformed by the Renewing of Our Minds 36
Week 13: Walking in Step With God 38

FEAR NOT

Week 14: Safety in the Storm 42
Week 15: God Stands With You 44
Week 16: Big Fears, Bigger God 46
Week 17: Defeating Fear With Courage 48
Week 18: Free From Fear of Man 50
Week 19: Seeing God's Angels Around You 52
Week 20: Divine Prison Break 54

STRETCH... GO BEYOND!

Week 21: Recovering Generational Inheritance ... 58
Week 22: Recovering What's Lost ... 60
Week 23: Healing From Trauma ... 62
Week 24: Failure Is Not Final ... 64
Week 25: Embrace a New Calling ... 66
Week 26: God Does Not Disqualify You ... 68

GET YOUR BATTLE STRATEGIES

Week 27: Praise Goes First ... 72
Week 28: Strength in the Unlikely ... 74
Week 29: Waiting for the Opportune Moment ... 76
Week 30: God Leads Us to the Impossible First ... 78
Week 31: Break Free From Sin ... 80
Week 32: God Is Bigger Than Your Giant ... 82
Week 33: Destroying the Enemy's Works ... 84

FIND HEALING & RESTORATION

Week 34: Realignment With Covenant Relationships ... 88
Week 35: God Heals All ... 90
Week 36: God's Restitution ... 92
Week 37: God Restores Your Rest ... 94
Week 38: The Joy of the Lord ... 96
Week 39: Renewing Strength ... 98
Week 40: Filled to the Brim With Hope ... 100
Week 41: Shalom Shalom ... 102
Week 42: Redeeming Time ... 104
Week 43: Prepare to Cross Over ... 106

DEVELOP AN EXPECTATION OF THE FUTURE

Week 44: Nothing Is Impossible for God................................110
Week 45: Blessed With Every Spiritual Blessing.....................112
Week 46: Above All That You Can Ask or Think.....................114
Week 47: Press Toward the Goal...116
Week 48: Strength for Every Season......................................118
Week 49: Empowered for Greater Works...............................120
Week 50: Faith That Sees...122
Week 51: Lean Not on Your Own Understanding....................124
Week 52: From Fear to Confidence!......................................126

Conclusion 128

References 129

INTRODUCTION

Are you ready to step boldly into the fullness of God's calling for your life?

Whether you're opening the Bible for the very first time or deepening a faith that has carried you for years, this prayer journal is your invitation to embrace the future with strength, hope and purpose. Over the next 52 weeks, you'll uncover powerful truths in Scripture that will equip you to break free from the fear, doubt, and limitations that may have held you back!

This is your moment to lay down deferred hope, disappointments, and regrets and to fully embrace the freedom and joy that come with walking in God's purpose for your life. This journal is designed to guide you through heartfelt reflections, prayers, and practical applications that will see your life and heart renewed.

Here's a truth to hold on to: God is with you every step of the way. He loves you unconditionally, He knows you completely, and calls you His own—no matter your struggles or imperfections. In these pages, you have the freedom to be completely real with Him. Trust in His grace and unfailing love to meet you where you are.

Come on this journey expectant, ready to grow, and willing to be changed. Whether you're laying a brand-new foundation of faith or building on the one you already have, this marks the start of something new. You are stepping into God's purpose and victory.

Heavenly Father,

You are generous and kind, mighty and powerful. I praise You for the work of Your hand and Your promises. As I embark on this journey, I pray You consistently remind me of Your goodness. I ask that You give me the strength to surrender to Your purposes for my life. May Your Spirit comfort and guide me. May Your presence empower and inspire me to walk out my faith for Your glory. Thank You for Your love and for the gift of Your Word. I love You. Amen.

SECTION One

EMBRACE NEW BEGINNINGS

This is your fresh start—a new beginning filled with hope and promise! We've all experienced disappointments, heartaches, and seasons that have left us feeling stuck or defeated. But you don't have to stay there. God is calling you up and into the life He has prepared for you. Imagine yourself walking hand in hand with the Holy Spirit, filled with unshakable peace, renewed purpose, and a confidence in your future that only God can give.

Does that feel out of reach? Do you wonder if your past mistakes or struggles disqualify you? Well, nothing is impossible for God. He can do far more than you can ask, think, or imagine, and He can make the impossible your reality.

God promises to walk beside you every step of the way. As you dive into this first section of the devotional, know that you are stepping into the new beginning God has lovingly prepared for you. Week by week, you'll be encouraged to release the burdens of the past, embrace the beauty of what's ahead, and fix your eyes on Jesus—the One who makes all things new. God's best is ahead.

WEEK 1:
HE IS MAKING A WAY FOR YOU

Read Isaiah 43:18–19
As you read, underline what God says He will do.

"Do not remember the former things, Nor consider the things of old. Behold, I will do a new thing, Now it shall spring forth; Shall you not know it? I will even make a road in the wilderness And rivers in the desert."

Reflect

We've all faced disappointments and heartbreak. It's easy to feel discouraged by these experiences. In this passage, God is encouraging His people not to dwell on the past but to open our hearts to the new thing He is doing. Even when it feels like nothing is changing, God is always at work. He is already making a way for you. He has plans you don't know about. If you're going through a challenging time today, know that God has not forgotten you. He's always working to redeem and restore even the most challenging circumstances in your life. He is able to make a road in the wilderness and rivers in the desert for you. Surrender the painful memories of the past to Him and trust that He is leading you toward a new beginning—one filled with hope, healing, and purpose. Let Him make a way for you.

What could change in your life if you put off defeat and walked the new road God has for you? These changes might be internal or external.

✲ _____

_____

Give Thanks

List 5 things you are thankful for in this moment.

✳ _____

_____

_____

_____

Pray

Offer God your thanks for the new beginning He has created for you. Ask for His help as you strive to walk in this freedom and hope. Writing your prayers down can help you remain focused and intentional, but feel free to pray however you feel comfortable.

Take Action

What steps can you take this week to remind yourself of the beginning God is offering you?

✳ _____

_____

_____

_____

WEEK 2:
REACH FORWARD TO THOSE THINGS AHEAD

Read Philippians 3:13–14
As you read, underline or highlight what Paul says he does.

"Brethren, I do not count myself to have apprehended; but one thing I do, forgetting those things which are behind and reaching forward to those things which are ahead, I press toward the goal for the prize of the upward call of God in Christ Jesus."

Reflection

Paul wrote this letter to the church at Philippi, which was a large city in Macedonia. When Paul was first establishing this church, he experienced resistance and hardship. He was thrown in jail and flogged. However, God used Paul's time in prison to save the guards. After being freed, the Philippian church was formed. Fast forward to Paul writing this letter, and he is in prison again. Knowing a little bit about Paul's experiences can give this passage deeper meaning. Despite his circumstances, this letter is filled with joy. Paul did not let his hardship defeat him. He wrote this letter to encourage the Philippian church. It can bring us encouragement today as well. Paul's words are a reminder that our lives can be sustained by God. We can follow Paul's example and not dwell on our pasts, but keep our eyes focused on Jesus instead.

What steps can you take to keep your eyes focused on Jesus instead of your past?

✸ _____

_____

Give Thanks

List 5 things you are thankful for in this moment.

✸ _____

_____

Pray

Write down a prayer, giving God your thanks and worship. Remember, your prayers can be simple, eloquent, long, or short.

✸ _____

_____

Take Action

What is one thing you believe God is leading you to do this week? Perhaps He is prompting you to reach out to a friend in need. Maybe He wants you to forgive somebody who has wronged you. Listen to the Holy Spirit's guidance.

✸ _____

_____

WEEK 3:
GOD WORKS ALL
THINGS FOR GOOD

Read Genesis 45:4–5
As you read, underline the actions of God.

"And Joseph said to his brothers, 'Please come near to me.' So they came near. Then he said: 'I am Joseph your brother, whom you sold into Egypt. But now, do not therefore be grieved or angry with yourselves because you sold me here; for God sent me before you to preserve life.'"

Reflect

In this passage, Joseph is speaking with his brothers—the brothers who betrayed him and sold him into slavery. They were anxious that Joseph might seek vengeance against them. Instead, Joseph was able to see God's bigger plan at work. While he was not excusing what they did, he realized that God had used them for good. Joseph's family was welcomed into Pharaoh's land where they established themselves and prospered. This led to Israel (a family of 70) growing to a nation of nearly 2 million! God's purposes are perfect. We may not fully understand God's plan in the moment, especially when those moments are difficult and painful. However, like Joseph, we can trust that God's sovereign plan will turn tragedy to triumph! God is able to use any circumstance for your good and His glory. On our hardest days, we can cling to this truth, and it can help us endure. Boldly proclaim that no matter what you are going through, God is using it for good!

Think of a trial or hardship you are currently facing. It could be something small or something very painful. How might God use this circumstance for good?

�֍ _____

_____

Give Thanks

List 5 things you are thankful for in this moment.

✶ _____

_____

Pray

Sometimes when we are in the midst of a trial, it can be difficult to see how God is working. In your prayer today, seek God's wisdom. Ask Him to give you perspective on how He is using the hard, painful things in your life for good. Write down your prayer below.

✶ _____

_____

Take Action

God often partners with us to turn things around for His glory. Reflect on the trial you are currently facing. What is one step you can take to give God glory in this circumstance?

✶ _____

_____

WEEK 4: FRUITFUL EVEN DURING AFFLICTION

Read Genesis 41:52
As you read, underline or highlight the meaning of Joseph's second son's name.

"And the name of the second he called Ephraim: 'For God has caused me to be fruitful in the land of my affliction.'"

Reflect

Joseph faced a lot of opposition, but that never stopped him from prospering and living out his God-given purpose. Scripture tells us that Joseph had favor with God. Whether he was a servant in Potiphar's house or a prisoner, Joseph was put in charge of those around him. After correctly interpreting Pharaoh's dream when no one else could, Joseph was promoted from slave to second in charge over all of Egypt. Talk about an amazing story of redemption! During trials and hardship, it is tempting to simply endure, but we can do so much more than that. With the help of God, we can prosper! There will be good days and bad days, but if you keep your eyes fixed on Jesus, you too can be fruitful in the land of your affliction. If He redeemed Joseph and brought restoration to his life, He will do the same for you!

How does Joseph's experience encourage you as you face trials and difficulties?

✳ _____

_____

_____

Give Thanks

List 5 things you are thankful for in this moment.

✳ _____

_____

_____

Pray

Prayer is a vital part of your relationship with God. Ask God to prosper you where you are today. No matter what obstacles you are facing, God is with you.

Take Action

God might enable us to be fruitful, but it also takes action on our part. What is one thing you can do this week to live out your purpose in Christ?

✳ _____

_____

_____

SECTION Two

RESET YOUR HEART

The Bible has a lot to say about the heart, and for good reason. Proverbs 4:23 reminds us that the heart is the wellspring of life, the source from which everything flows! Many of us might associate our heart solely with emotions, but we see in Scripture that the heart is so much more than that. Did you know our hearts can think, plan, and make decisions?

Perhaps there is some truth to that phrase, "follow your heart," but only when your heart is aligned with God's truth. Over the next few weeks, we are going to dive deep into matters of the heart. Why? Because the condition of your heart matters deeply to God. It is the foundation of your relationship with Him and the compass that guides your life. A broken or bruised heart doesn't disqualify you; God specializes in healing and restoring hearts. But here's the key—we have to be vulnerable and let God in.

Are you ready to experience renewal and allow God to work in the hidden places of your heart? Let's get started!

WEEK 5: HEALING COMES AS YOU FORGIVE

Read Ephesians 4:31–32
As you read, underline how we are to forgive one another.

"Let all bitterness, wrath, anger, clamor, and evil speaking be put away from you, with all malice. And be kind to one another, tenderhearted, forgiving one another, even as God in Christ forgave you."

Reflect

Have you ever heard the phrase, "hurt people hurt people"? It refers to how we as human beings can perpetuate cycles of pain and trauma. When we feel put down, we tend to do the same to others. Have you ever responded to hurt with gossip or hateful words? Have you ever sought to get even? With Jesus, we can end this cycle and experience healing. Our sin hurts God, but instead of hurting us back, He chooses to forgive. He gives us new mercy and grace each day. So much can improve in life if our words and actions reflect a grateful and forgiven heart. Releasing bitterness and anger is a difficult step in our journey with God, but He can give you the strength! It starts with celebrating the fact that you are forgiven by God! From this, forgiveness of others and personal healing can flow. Through the Holy Spirit, God can renew and restore your relationships. You can end the cycle of hurt and start a new cycle—one of love!

What steps can you take to forgive the people in your life who have hurt you?

✻ _____

_____

Give Thanks

List 5 things you are thankful for in this moment.

✻ _____

_____

Pray

In your prayer today, invite God to heal your broken heart. He cares for you and wants to bring you peace. Also ask God for the strength to forgive others. If needed, you can repent of times when you inflicted pain on those around you. Your Creator forgives you. Feel free to write your prayer in the space provided.

✻ _____

_____

Take Action

What are a few acts of kindness you can practice to those around you this week?

✻ _____

_____

WEEK 6: CASTING LIGHT ON OUR SHADOWS

Read Hebrews 4:12–13
As you read, underline what the Word of God discerns.

"For the word of God is living and powerful, and sharper than any two-edged sword, piercing even to the division of soul and spirit, and of joints and marrow, and is a discerner of the thoughts and intents of the heart. And there is no creature hidden from His sight, but all things are naked and open to the eyes of Him to whom we must give account.

Reflect

As you journey with God, there are often times when you need to look inward. Your own heart can feel mysterious to you, but God sees the core of who you are. It might feel vulnerable and uncomfortable knowing that God is aware of your every thought, desire, and intent. Perhaps you fear rejection or judgment. There is so much we keep hidden from others and even things we refuse to acknowledge to ourselves. We might try to hide things from God, but He knows us intimately. Despite the shadows of your heart, God loves you more than you can imagine. His Holy Spirit can help you look inward and shed light on your blind spots. He can guide you in aligning your heart to the heart of God so that you can become more like Christ. This process can be challenging, but through it, your heart can know peace.

What habits can you develop to align your heart more closely to God's?

✱ _____

_____

_____

Give Thanks

List 5 things you are thankful for in this moment.

✱ _____

_____

_____

Pray

You can be honest with God in your prayers, knowing that He loves you unconditionally. Ask Him to reveal the hidden places of your heart—the unacknowledged thoughts and motives—so that you can find healing through His Holy Spirit.

Take Action

Our words have power! Write a declaration stating that the core of your desires, thoughts, and feelings will come into alignment with God's heart. Memorize this declaration this week.

✱ _____

_____

_____

WEEK 7: CREATING A NEW HEART

Read Psalm 51:10
As you read, underline the two requests of the psalmist.

"Create in me a clean heart, O God, And renew a steadfast spirit within me."

Reflect

In this verse, David is asking God to create in him a clean heart. This prayer is born from deep repentance after his sin with Bathsheba and the devastating choices he made to cover it up. David doesn't simply ask for forgiveness—he pleads for transformation. The Hebrew word for "create" is the same used in Genesis to describe God's creation of the world, something only He can do. David recognizes that his heart is beyond self-repair; he needs God to make it completely new, clean, and aligned with His will. This verse reminds us that no matter how far we've strayed or how broken we feel, God can restore us. We might not have committed the same sins as David, but Scripture says that every way of a man is right in his own eyes but that God weighs the heart (Proverbs 21:2). You might not feel like your heart is always clean or pure, but God can create in you a clean heart. You can make David's words your own as you call out to God knowing that everything He creates is *good*. No matter what you've done, He can create in you a heart that not only seeks Him but delights in His will. It might be painful and vulnerable at times, but it is worth it!

What steps can you take to open your heart up to God more each day?

* _____

Give Thanks

List 5 things you are thankful for in this moment.

* _____

Pray

Use this psalm to inspire your prayer today, asking God to create in you a clean heart. It can be helpful to write down your prayers so that you can look back on them one day.

* _____

Take Action

Sometime this week, read Ezekiel 36:25, meditating on this amazing promise from God.

* _____

WEEK 8:
A FULLY DEVOTED HEART

Read Matthew 5:8
As you read, underline who is blessed.

"Blessed are the pure in heart, For they shall see God."

Reflect

Our hearts shape every part of who we are—our actions, motives, emotions, and even our desires. When Jesus says the "pure of heart," He is not just talking about moral perfection. He is speaking about a singleness of heart, a heart fully devoted to Him. The word "blessed" here means far more than just happiness; it describes a deep, unshakable joy that comes from being in relationship with God. When our hearts are divided or distracted by worldly concerns, our thoughts and affections become scattered. We may begin to put our trust in fleeting things: success, relationships, possessions, even ourselves. This can steal our peace and joy and leave us spiritually stagnant. None of us are perfect, and Jesus knows that. Purity of heart is never about not failing; it's about returning to God daily, allowing Him to cleanse us and realign our hearts. Through faith in Jesus, our hearts are continually renewed. So let's pursue purity of heart, not by striving but surrendering to the One who purifies us. This is the amazing promise from God for those who are pure in heart—that we will see Him!

In what areas in life are you and your heart being pulled away from God?

✻ _____

_____

_____

Give Thanks

List 5 things you are thankful for in this moment.

✻ _____

_____

_____

Pray

Spend time today in prayer, asking God to give you a singleness of heart. Invite His guidance, conviction, and encouragement into your life today. Remember, your prayers do not have to be eloquent; you can talk to God like a friend.

Take Action

Revisit your response to today's reflection question. What can you do in these circumstances to remain faithful?

✻ _____

_____

_____

SECTION Three

SECURE YOUR GATES

Let's take a closer look at five key areas that deeply influence your spiritual journey: your eyes, your ears, your mouth, your mind, and your feet. These aren't just parts of your body—they're gateways to your soul and spirit. Think about it: What you see, hear, speak, think, and the paths you choose to walk can either build and nurture your faith or pull you off course.

When your spiritual gates are aligned with God, they become channels for His goodness to flow into your life. But when left unguarded, they can open doors to distractions, fears, and decisions that lead us away from His perfect plan. That's why securing these gates is so vital to your journey of faith.

Over the next few weeks, we will explore each one to uncover practical and powerful ways to align it with God's plan of redemption. Invite God into every part of your being. You can do this, trusting that God's plan for you is good and perfect.

WEEK 9: HEALING OUR BLIND SPOTS

Read Luke 18:40–43
As you read, underline what the man requested of Jesus.

"So Jesus stood still and commanded him to be brought to Him. And when he had come near, He asked him, saying, 'What do you want Me to do for you?' He said, 'Lord, that I may receive my sight.' Then Jesus said to him, 'Receive your sight; your faith has made you well.' And immediately he received his sight, and followed Him, glorifying God. And all the people, when they saw it, gave praise to God."

Reflect

This passage reveals a profound spiritual truth through the lens of physical healing. The blind man desired to see—physically. But what he received from Jesus was far more than physical vision. He received spiritual sight that transformed his entire life. In an instant, his eyes opened, and he saw not only the physical world around him but his Savior. Immediately after being healed, this man committed his life to Jesus and followed Him, leaving behind the spiritual darkness that once defined his life. Just like this man, we all have blind spots, places in our hearts and lives where we struggle to see Jesus clearly. Jesus can bring clarity, healing and a renewed sense of purpose to those areas. Maybe you feel like the blind man—stuck, overlooked, and unable to see a way forward. Take heart! Jesus sees you and hears you. He is ready to meet you where you are. Turn to Him and let Him help you see through the lens of faith and possibility.

What are some ways you can fix your eyes on Jesus?

✳ _____

_____

_____

Give Thanks

List 5 things you are thankful for in this moment.

✳ _____

_____

_____

Pray

As you pray, ask the Lord to remove any scales you might have over your eyes—any blind spots or things blocking your view of Jesus. Ask God to bring you clarity and the boldness to follow Him.

Take Action

After being healed, the man in this story not only followed Jesus, but glorified Him! How can you glorify Jesus this week with your words or actions?

✳ _____

_____

_____

WEEK 10: RESTORING OUR SPIRITUAL HEARING

Read Mark 7:32–34
As you read, underline Jesus' words.

"Then they brought to Him one who was deaf and had an impediment in his speech, and they begged Him to put His hand on him. And He took him aside from the multitude, and put His fingers in his ears, and He spat and touched his tongue. Then, looking up to heaven, He sighed, and said to him, 'Ephphatha,' that is, 'Be opened.'"

Reflect

Last week, we reflected on Jesus healing blind eyes. In today's story, we see Jesus restore hearing. These healings are more than accounts of physical miracles—they convey profound truths about our lives. There is a reason Jesus often healed those who were blind or deaf. Our eyes and ears are critical gateways to spiritual growth and life! They shape how we perceive God's truth and respond to His calling. From social media to endless newsfeeds, there are many voices competing for your attention. What and who you choose to listen to will greatly impact your life and faith. While you can't tune everything out, you can develop the ability to recognize Jesus when He is speaking to you. His Holy Spirit is with you and in you, guiding, comforting, convicting, and giving wisdom. Are you listening? If you find it hard to recognize the voice of God in your life, Jesus can restore your spiritual hearing just as He physically did for this man in the story.

Among all the noise in your life, what little things can you do each day to create quiet moments and intentionally listen to the Lord?

* _____
  _____
  _____

Give Thanks

List 5 things you are thankful for in this moment.

* _____
  _____
  _____

Pray

Begin and end your time in prayer today with silence. Silence can feel awkward because we aren't used to it. When your mind wonders, that's okay. Bring your thoughts back to God and use this time to focus on God's Holy Spirit within you.

Take Action

Make it a goal this week to ask the Lord to restore your hearing every day. Ask Him to enable you to hear Him clearly.

* _____
  _____
  _____

WEEK 11: THE POWER OF OUR WORDS

Read Psalm 141:3
As you read, underline what the psalmist compares his mouth to.

"Set a guard, O Lord, over my mouth; Keep watch over the door of my lips."

Reflect

Our words hold incredible power. They shape the world around us and the lives of those we touch. The book of Proverbs reminds us that our words carry the weight of life and death. What we say matters deeply! God spoke the universe into existence with His voice, and as His image-bearers, our words carry a creative force as well. They can create, heal, build bridges, worship, and inspire. But they can also wound, divide, or destroy. The psalmist understood this truth and prayed a simple but profound prayer asking God to guard his mouth. When we invite God to guide our words, they can be used to bring encouragement, hope and life to every situation. By declaring His truth over our lives and circumstances, we step into a place where our words align with His will and His purposes. Today, ask God to help you use your words to inspire, uplift, and declare faith!

How do you struggle with matters of the mouth (things like gossip, negative self-talk, or lying)? How might your life change if you invited God to guard your words?

* _____
  _____
  _____

Give Thanks

List 5 things you are thankful for in this moment.

* _____
  _____
  _____

Pray

One way to surrender our lips to the Lord is to fill our mouths with praise! Use your time in prayer today to worship God for who He is and all He has done. Journal as well as pray out loud today if you are able.

Take Action

A great verse to memorize is Psalm 19:14. Use this week to meditate on the words and memorize it, taking this psalm to heart.

* _____
  _____
  _____

WEEK 12: TRANSFORMED BY THE RENEWING OF OUR MINDS

Read Romans 12:2
As you read, underline how we are called to be transformed.

"And do not be conformed to this world, but be transformed by the renewing of your mind, that you may prove what is that good and acceptable and perfect will of God."

Reflect

In this verse, Paul tells us not to conform to the world's way of thinking or living but to allow God to transform us through the renewing of our minds. But what does this mean? It helps to look at the word "transformed." This is the same word used at Jesus' transfiguration when He appeared different—radiant and glowing with the power of God. This verse tells us that the same is possible for us. In order to see outward transformation, we need inward renewal. The word "renewing" here only occurs twice in the New Testament, and it refers to something becoming not just new and different but also superior. The word "perfect" is often translated "mature" or "complete" but also encapsulates the idea of having reached the goal or purpose that was originally intended. When we continually yield our minds to God, we will not only begin to understand His will for our lives, we will also become all that He has purposed us to be. This is an amazing promise from God.

In Philippians 4:6, Paul tells us that God can guard our minds. What kind of limiting, worldly mindsets do you need to be guarded from?

* _____
_____

Give Thanks

List 5 things you are thankful for in this moment.

* _____
_____

Pray

Ask God to renew your mind. Ask for Him to reveal where you might be stuck with limiting thoughts and seek His comfort and help. Writing down your prayers can help keep you intentional and focused.

* _____
_____

Take Action

We cannot simply release old, limiting mindsets. We need to replace them with new ones that speak to God's power and our victory through Jesus! What empowering truths can you meditate on this week?

* _____
_____

WEEK 13: WALKING IN STEP WITH GOD

Read Proverbs 4:26–27
As you read, underline what God did for the psalmist.

"Ponder the path of your feet, And let all your ways be established. Do not turn to the right or the left; Remove your foot from evil."

Reflect

To ponder means to consider carefully or weigh a matter. It also means to make level or smooth. The "path" of your feet in this verse refers to your way of life and conduct. These verses remind us that the choices we make daily shape not only our journey but also our destination. When was the last time you truly reflected on how you are living? Like Paul in 1 Thessalonians 5:21–22, Solomon tells us to examine everything carefully, to hold fast to what is good and to stay far from evil. We need to watch our steps daily, or we could drift away from God's best for us. Unguided steps carry us toward sin and selfish desires. The good news is that God is with you, leading you, and establishing your steps. He promises to help you overcome challenges and even puts the enemy under your feet! However, this also requires action on your part. God might be guiding, but you must have the courage to step out in faith, knowing that His plan can be counted on.

What kinds of things distract you from the path God has put you on? What can you do to remain in step with Him?

✳ _____
   _____
   _____

Give Thanks

List 5 things you are thankful for in this moment.

✳ _____
   _____
   _____

Pray

The Lord has established your steps for the days ahead. Ask for His plan to be made clear to you. Seek His Holy Spirit's discernment and guidance. Ask Him to give you the strength to walk in step with the path He has made for you.

Take Action

List one way you can listen more closely to God's guidance, one way you can step out in obedience, and one way you can resist evil. Make a commitment to do these things this week.

✳ _____
   _____
   _____

SECTION Four

FEAR NOT

Do not fear is a command that occurs more than 400 times in the Bible, and there is a reason we see these words so much. It is natural for us to experience fear. The world is full of risk and opposition. God commands us to not fear because He is greater than anything we will face. Not only is God capable of helping us and delivering us, but He is with us each and every moment. He promises never to leave our side. We see time after time that God comes through for His people.

Breaking free of fear might seem like a daunting command, but it is possible with God. Over the next few weeks, we will explore how we can overcome fear with God's strength.

WEEK 14: SAFETY IN THE STORM

Read Psalm 46:1–3
As you read, underline what the psalmist says God is.

"God is our refuge and strength, A very present help in trouble. Therefore we will not fear, Even though the earth be removed, And though the mountains be carried into the midst of the sea; Though its waters roar and be troubled, Though the mountains shake with its swelling."

Reflect

A refuge is a place of shelter, safety, and security. When troubles come, we may run to seek refuge in all sorts of places: in finances, in relationships, in our social lives, and maybe even in food. While some of these things are not bad, when the storms of life come crashing down on us, we can be left feeling exposed and vulnerable. However, God is a safe hiding place. Take a moment to think about what brings you fear or anxiety. Now, imagine God as your refuge, shielding you from those things. Imagine Him giving you strength and helping you face the storms of life. His very present help means He's already in the midst of your troubles. God's refuge and strength is available to you right here, right now. Life is not guaranteed to be easy without obstacles or hardship, but God promises that He will protect and help you! He promises never to leave your side.

How does this verse impact the way you respond to hardship or difficulties in life?

✳ _____

_____

_____

Give Thanks

List 5 things you are thankful for in this moment.

✳ _____

_____

_____

Pray

Seek God's refuge today in prayer. Praise Him for the strength He promises to give you and offer your thanks for His safe haven.

Take Action

Shelter will only protect us if we enter it. What can you do this week to enter into the refuge of the Lord?

✳ _____

_____

_____

WEEK 15: GOD STANDS WITH YOU

Read 2 Timothy 4:16–18
As you read, underline what the Lord did and will do.

"At my first defense no one stood with me, but all forsook me. May it not be charged against them. But the Lord stood with me and strengthened me, so that the message might be preached fully through me, and that all the Gentiles might hear. Also I was delivered out of the mouth of the lion. And the Lord will deliver me from every evil work and preserve me for His heavenly kingdom. To Him be glory forever and ever. Amen!"

Reflect

In this passage, Paul reflects on how He was forced to face a trial without the support of his friends or fellow believers. Have you ever felt abandoned in life? Have you been betrayed or disappointed? These experiences can cause us to fear abandonment and we may be slow to trust anyone else but ourselves. However, this was not the case with Paul. He knew that God had never left his side! Because Paul did not give in to fear and despair, God's message was able to be preached through him! In moments when you feel alone or fearful that God will abandon you like other people have, remember His promise that He will never leave you. God cannot break His promises. No matter what evil plan the enemy throws your way, God will deliver you!

How can letting go of the fear of abandonment lead to spiritual growth?

* _____
  _____
  _____

Give Thanks

List 5 things you are thankful for in this moment.

* _____
  _____
  _____

Pray

Pray for God to make His presence clear to you—especially when you feel alone. Thank Him for the ways in which He has been there for you in the past and how He will continue to deliver you from the enemy's schemes.

Take Action

List some ways you can remind yourself of God's faithfulness and deliverance.

* _____
  _____
  _____

WEEK 10: BIG FEARS, BIGGER GOD

Read Numbers 14:9
As you read, underline the word "fear" each time it appears.

"Only do not rebel against the Lord, nor fear the people of the land, for they are our bread; their protection has departed from them, and the Lord is with us. Do not fear them."

Reflect

God had promised Israel land for them to establish themselves in. When they finally arrived at that land, they saw giants living there and feared for their lives. They had seen the Lord miraculously deliver them from Egypt and supernaturally provide for them along their journey. Yet unbelief gave in to fear and, literally at the threshold of their promise, they decided that Egypt and dying elsewhere was better than obeying God. In verse 9, Joshua reminds them not to give in to fear and that God is with them. Fear can cause us to disobey God. God might be calling us to some big things—intimidating things. Instead of letting fear drive us away from God's calling, we need to remind ourselves that He is always faithful. He is able to sustain us and provide for us, even in the face of seemingly insurmountable odds. He will give us victory over our enemies. Declare today that the giants you face are bread in light of God's promises, faithfulness, and strength!

What habits can you develop that will help you rely on God as you face obstacles and opposition?

✸ _____

Give Thanks

List 5 things you are thankful for in this moment.

✸ _____

Pray

Lift up any fears you have, surrendering them to the Lord. Ask for His help in facing your giants and declaring them as bread. Write your prayer in the space below.

✸ _____

Take Action

What might God be calling you to this week? What can you do to overcome any fears you have surrounding this?

✸ _____

WEEK 17: DEFEATING FEAR WITH COURAGE

Read Joshua 1:9
As you read, underline what God commands Joshua to be and not be.

"Have I not commanded you? Be strong and of good courage; do not be afraid, nor be dismayed, for the Lord your God is with you wherever you go."

Reflect

Joshua faced a daunting task after the death of Moses: Lead the Israelites into the Promised Land. He knew that along the way he would face great opposition and battle. Joshua had every reason to be afraid. However, God encouraged Joshua not to let his fear stop him from fulfilling his call. God calls us all in unique ways, but many calls are left unanswered because of fear. Obedience can be scary, but instead of fear, we can put on courage. Why? Because God is there by our side! Nothing is too hard, too scary, or too complicated for God. Fear has a way of stopping us on our tracks. But like Joshua, you can be strong and walk in obedience to what God has called you to.

What can you do to help you move forward when you feel stuck or frozen with fear?

✻ _____

_____

_____

Give Thanks

List 5 things you are thankful for in this moment.

✻ _____

_____

_____

Pray

Ask for God to give you strength and courage. Praise Him for never leaving your side and for giving you purpose. Seek God's wisdom as you strive to live out this purpose.

Take Action

Just before this verse, God tells Joshua to meditate on the Word. Spend some time this week meditating and memorizing Joshua 1:9.

✻ _____

_____

_____

WEEK 18: FREE FROM FEAR OF MAN

Read Jeremiah 1:7–8
As you read, underline what the Lord says not to fear.

"But the Lord said to me: 'Do not say, "I am a youth," For you shall go to all to whom I send you, And whatever I command you, you shall speak. Do not be afraid of their faces, For I am with you to deliver you,' says the Lord."

Reflect

In this story, God calls Jeremiah to be a prophet. Jeremiah expressed doubt that anyone would listen to him because of his age. Many of us experience similar doubts when God calls us to step out in faith. We might worry about what people will think or that we are not qualified. We might fear failure. However, when God calls us, He will provide a way and give us strength. Later in his ministry, Jeremiah vividly contrasts two ways of living. He declares that those who trust in men are like a tree planted in the parched desert, cursed. But those who trust in the Lord are like a tree planted by a river, fearless and unshakable. Which would you rather be? If you want to break off your fear of men and walk in the goodness God has set before you, remember that God is trustworthy and will never call you to something He will not help you achieve.

What does "fear of man" look like in your own life? What might change in your life if you broke free of these fears?

✻ _____

_____

Give Thanks

List 5 things you are thankful for in this moment.

✻ _____

_____

Pray

Admit to God how you fear other people and what they think. He knows your struggles and loves you unconditionally. Ask for His empowerment and strength. Write your prayer in the space below.

✻ _____

_____

Take Action

God called Jeremiah to be a prophet. What is God calling you to do? Write down how you can walk in obedience this week and make a commitment to do so.

✻ _____

_____

WEEK 19: SEEING GOD'S ANGELS AROUND YOU

Read 2 Kings 6:16–17
As you read, underline the prayer of Elisha.

"So he answered, 'Do not fear, for those who are with us are more than those who are with them.' And Elisha prayed, and said, 'Lord, I pray, open his eyes that he may see.' Then the Lord opened the eyes of the young man, and he saw. And behold, the mountain was full of horses and chariots of fire all around Elisha."

Reflect

Elisha was a prophet in the kingdom of Israel. We can learn so much from his example as he lived each day aware of God's presence with him. In this story, they were surrounded by great armies. Elisha's servant became fearful, but Elisha knew something he did not. God's angels were with them. Sometimes we are like the man in this story, blind to God's angels that encamp all around us. But when we are aware of God's presence and protection, our fear disappears. No matter what opposition you face or what hardship you endure, God's angels are with you! These angels are there to help you overcome obstacles. If you need help seeing them, make Elisha's prayer your own. Ask God to open your eyes and give you courage. We can have confidence that He will answer this prayer!

How might being aware of God's angels and presence around you impact the way you handle opposition and difficulties?

✸ _____

_____

_____

Give Thanks

List 5 things you are thankful for in this moment.

✸ _____

_____

_____

Pray

Pray for God to open your eyes to His angels! Remember your prayers can be eloquent or short and simple.

Take Action

This week, commit to reading all of 2 Kings 6. It is a wonderful story about depending on God's presence and aid during opposition.

✸ _____

_____

_____

WEEK 20:
DIVINE PRISON BREAK

Read Acts 12:11
As you read, underline what the Lord did.

"And when Peter had come to himself, he said, 'Now I know for certain that the Lord has sent His angel, and has delivered me from the hand of Herod and from all the expectation of the Jewish people.'"

Reflect

In this incredible story, Peter finds himself locked away in prison for boldly following Jesus. Meanwhile, the church refuses to give up hope. They unite in constant, fervent prayer for his release. Then, in a miraculous act, God sends an angel to break Peter out of prison! When Peter finally realizes it wasn't a dream, he is quick to give glory and credit to God for being his deliverer. You might not be in a literal prison, but you likely encounter things in life that try to limit you or cause you to fear. The enemy wants nothing more than for you to believe there's no way out, to keep you trapped in despair. But do not forget who your Deliverer is. God's power knows no limits and He uses your prayers to bring about His sovereign will. Our prayers are powerful as they allow us to partner with God and His perfect plan. Just as Peter experienced divine deliverance, you too can trust that God is there to save you from the hand of the enemy. Nobody is more powerful than the Lord!

What things do you need freedom from—what fears, opposition, or chains? How can you remind yourself to pray over these circumstances each day?

✱ _____
 _____
 _____

Give Thanks

List 5 things you are thankful for in this moment.

✱ _____
 _____
 _____

Pray

Pray over the circumstances you listed in the reflection question. Ask for God's deliverance and offer Him all the praise and glory.

Take Action

Remembering how God has come through for you in the past is a great way to build your trust in the present. Each day this week, take a moment to give God credit and glory for the ways in which He has delivered you.

✱ _____
 _____
 _____

SECTION Five

STRETCH... GO BEYOND!

They say comfort is a quiet killer. Being too comfortable physically (never exercising or sitting all day) can lead to physical limitations. The same is true spiritually. While we often cling to what's familiar, comfort is not where growth happens. To grow spiritually, we must stretch beyond what feels safe or easy.

When we step out in faith and obedience, God uses us to accomplish extraordinary things for His kingdom. Growth is not always comfortable, but without it, we stay stuck—perhaps in old patterns, fear, or places far below the abundant life God has for us.

Over the next few weeks, we will explore what it looks like to move beyond our failures, our trauma, and even our limited understanding and step into the victories God has already planned for us.

Week 21: Recovering Generational Inheritance

Read Joshua 11:23
As you read, underline what Joshua gave to Israel.

"So Joshua took the whole land, according to all that the Lord had said to Moses; and Joshua gave it as an inheritance to Israel according to their divisions by their tribes. Then the land rested from war."

Reflect

In Joshua 11:23, we see God's faithfulness in action. Through Joshua, God fulfilled His promise of giving the Israelites a great and plentiful land. This land would become a blessing passed down from generation to generation. This is not just about land; it is about legacy, provision, and God's unwavering commitment to His people. You too have a generational blessing and inheritance. Maybe you are already walking in this blessing. If so, go further to establish a legacy for those who will come after you. Or perhaps you feel this blessing has been lost along the way. The good news? It is never too late to reclaim it. Ask God for wisdom and strategies to recover what's been stolen or forgotten. As Christians, we are adopted into God's family and are heirs to His kingdom. Our ultimate inheritance is in Heaven, but we are not without blessings here on earth. When we reclaim our generational blessings, we create a legacy to pass along to those who come after us just as Joshua did.

What generational inheritance has been passed to you? How can you live out this blessing?

* _____
  _____
  _____

Give Thanks

List 5 things you are thankful for in this moment.

* _____
  _____
  _____

Pray

Ask God to establish the work of your hands as you seek to participate in His calling for you. Ask that He multiplies your efforts and that your light creates a lasting impact.

Take Action

Write down what kind of legacy you wish to leave to your family and future believers. Search for ways to work toward this legacy this week.

* _____
  _____
  _____

WEEK 22: RECOVERING WHAT'S LOST

Read 2 Kings 4:32–35
As you read, underline the word "stretched" when it appears.

"When Elisha came into the house, there was the child, lying dead on his bed. He went in therefore, shut the door behind the two of them, and prayed to the Lord. And he went up and lay on the child, and put his mouth on his mouth, his eyes on his eyes, and his hands on his hands; and he stretched himself out on the child, and the flesh of the child became warm. He returned and walked back and forth in the house, and again went up and stretched himself out on him; then the child sneezed seven times, and the child opened his eyes."

Reflect

This is a powerful story of faith, persistence, and God's faithfulness. The mother in this story was unable to have a child, but God promised her a son and fulfilled this promise. Years later, tragedy struck, and her son died. But she did not settle or accept this fate. By laying him on the bed of Elisha, God's prophet, this woman prepared her son for resurrection, not burial. She believed that God could and would restore what seemed permanently lost. Elisha's repeated act of stretching himself over the boy is the same posture of faith we need to exercise as we reclaim the premature death of God's promises over our lives. This story is a beautiful reminder that God is always faithful to His promises, even when circumstances try to tell us otherwise. When His promises seem delayed or even dead, we can go to the Lord, confidently knowing that He desires to restore what is lost. Trust Him to fulfill every promise in His perfect time!

What promises of God feel lost in your life? How can you stretch out in faith for these promises?

✳ _____

_____

_____

Give Thanks

List 5 things you are thankful for in this moment.

✳ _____

_____

_____

Pray

Prayer is a vital part of our spiritual journey. It allows us to grow in relationship with God. Use this time to reflect on God's promises and pray against any death assignments on your life, family, or purpose.

Take Action

Write down any broken or lost dreams you have. Make a commitment to surrender these to the Lord each day this week, seeking His restoration and hope.

✳ _____

_____

_____

WEEK 23: HEALING FROM TRAUMA

Read 1 Samuel 30:8, 19–20
As you read, underline the words "recover/recovered" when it appears.

"So David inquired of the Lord, saying, 'Shall I pursue this troop? Shall I overtake them?' And He answered him, 'Pursue, for you shall surely overtake them and without fail recover all'… And nothing of theirs was lacking, either small or great, sons or daughters, spoil or anything which they had taken from them; David recovered all. Then David took all the flocks and herds they had driven before those other livestock, and said, 'This is David's spoil.'"

Reflect

Before David's inquiry, Israel had suffered a great loss. The enemy had raided his camp, burned it to the ground, and taken their sons, daughters, and wives captive. Overwhelmed by grief, David and his men wept until they had no strength left. To make matters worse, David's men, consumed by grief and anger, spoke of stoning him. But David did not stay in that place of despair. Instead, he turned to the only source of true strength—*he strengthened himself in the Lord*. Then he sought God's guidance on how to recover his losses. With God's word to pursue, David led his men into battle, overtook the enemy, and recovered *everything*. Experiencing great loss has a tendency to stop us in our tracks, but with the help of God, we can move beyond this trauma. While there is a time to mourn, we go forward knowing that our story does not end in defeat. Your story does not end in defeat. Like David, you can ask for God's guidance, trust in His promises, and claim victory in the name of Christ!

What loss are you grieving right now? What would restoration look like in this circumstance?

✵ _____

_____

_____

Give Thanks

List 5 things you are thankful for in this moment.

✵ _____

_____

_____

Pray

Ask God to heal your broken heart and restore your hope. Seek His guidance on how to heal from your traumatic experiences.

Take Action

Write 1 Peter 5:10 on a sticky note or an index card. Put this in a place you will see every day—for example, on your mirror or work desk. Make an effort this week to meditate on this promise from God, taking it to heart.

✵ _____

_____

_____

WEEK 24: FAILURE IS NOT FINAL

Read Luke 5:5–6.
As you read, underline what motivated Simon to let his net down.

"But Simon answered and said to Him, 'Master, we have toiled all night and caught nothing; nevertheless at Your word I will let down the net.' And when they had done this, they caught a great number of fish, and their net was breaking."

Reflect

Simon had lost hope that they would catch any fish. Their efforts so far had failed. Even though he was tired and doubtful, he obeyed Jesus' call to cast the net one more time. The result? Incredible success and abundance! Failure is a part of life, but it does not define us. Past failures do not determine our futures. Jesus has placed a calling and purpose on your life. God's calling on your life does not change. Each setback is an opportunity for your faith to grow stronger, for you to rise beyond your last defeat. The secret lies in staying anchored to Jesus. Listen closely to His voice and at His word, step out in obedience and cast your net again. Do so with hope and confidence in the God's purposes for your life. Trust Him because with God, failure is never the final word.

How do you relate to Simon in this story? What might God be calling you to try again despite past failure?

✳ _____

_____

_____

Give Thanks

List 5 things you are thankful for in this moment.

✳ _____

_____

_____

Pray

Ask God to give you encouragement and hope. Ask Him to help you step out in obedience despite previous failures and trust in His plan and purpose for your life.

Take Action

Simon let down his net one more time because Jesus called him to. What can you do this week to better hear Christ's calling and guidance?

✳ _____

_____

_____

WEEK 25: EMBRACE A NEW CALLING

Read Luke 5:10–11.
As you read, underline what Simon, James, and John did in response to Jesus' words.

"And so also were James and John, the sons of Zebedee, who were partners with Simon. And Jesus said to Simon, 'Do not be afraid. From now on you will catch men.' So when they had brought their boats to land, they forsook all and followed Him."

Reflect

Last week, we read what happened right before this. Despite spending all night fishing and catching nothing, Simon obeyed Jesus to let down his net one more time. The result was a plentiful catch! Simon, James, and John were fishermen. They believed that they would fish their entire lives, just like their fathers before them. However, God was doing a new thing in their lives through Jesus. Jesus called them to walk away from their current calling and pick up another. Your purpose in life can change and evolve. In order to remain in step with the Holy Spirit, you need to stretch beyond your current understanding of your calling. God might be prompting you to go beyond and do something new. You can be obedient, knowing that God will equip you.

Following Jesus and abiding in Him is important as you seek to understand where He is calling you. How can you abide in Jesus each day?

✻ _____

_____

_____

Give Thanks

List 5 things you are thankful for in this moment.

✻ _____

_____

_____

Pray

Seek the clarity and wisdom of the Lord today. Ask Him to make His calling for you clear and that He will give you strength to obey.

Take Action

What can you do this week to let go of any preconceived notions about your calling and follow God's lead?

✻ _____

_____

_____

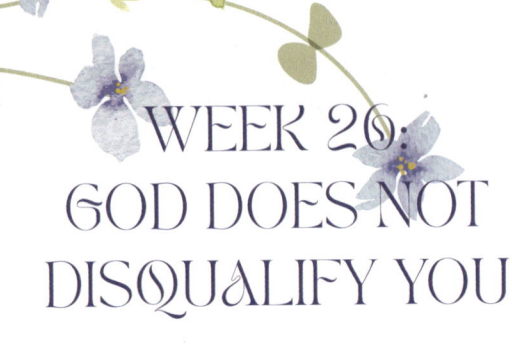

WEEK 20: GOD DOES NOT DISQUALIFY YOU

Read Luke 22:31–32.
As you read, underline what Jesus prays for Simon.

"And the Lord said, 'Simon, Simon! Indeed, Satan has asked for you, that he may sift you as wheat. But I have prayed for you, that your faith should not fail; and when you have returned to Me, strengthen your brethren.'"

Reflect

Simon, who would later be called Peter, is a powerful example of God's grace and redemption. This is the same Peter who boldly declared his loyalty to Jesus only to deny Him three times in His darkest hour. Yet, Simon's story did not end in failure. His faith wavered, but he returned to Christ. Not only that, the resurrected Jesus entrusted Peter with a calling that would change the world. What about you? Simon's weakness did not disqualify him from being used by God, and neither do yours! Perhaps you believe that you have disappointed God. Perhaps you believe the lie that God cannot use you because of your failures. Scripture tells us that Jesus is praying on your behalf. He knows your struggles, He sees your weakness, and He still calls you. Your shortcomings are not obstacles to God's plans—they are opportunities for His power to shine. He redeemed Simon and gave him a destiny beyond his imagination. He can do the same for you. God is not finished with you yet. Your story, like Peter's, can become a testimony of grace, restoration, and divine purpose!

How does knowing that Jesus prays for you impact your faith?

* _____
 _____
 _____

Give Thanks

List 5 things you are thankful for in this moment.

* _____
 _____
 _____

Pray

Pray for the restoration of your hope and purpose. Thank God for never giving up on you and for the strength He gives.

Take Action

What are some ways you can return to the Lord this week?

* _____
 _____
 _____

SECTION Six

GET YOUR BATTLE STRATEGIES

Life is full of battles, and while they challenge us, they also shape us. Without battles, we would never know what it means to overcome. Without challenges, there would be no testimony, no miracles, and no opportunity to experience the power of God in action. What if the battle you're facing right now is connected to your breakthrough or promotion?

An army never charges into battle without a strategy, and neither should we. The Bible reminds us not to be ignorant of the enemy's schemes but to be prepared. Scripture is filled with stories of triumph and divine wisdom, offering us strategies on how to navigate life's toughest moments and overcome them.

Sometimes God's plans can seem unconventional, even impossible from our perspective. But time and again, His ways prove higher than our own. As you face obstacles, trust in God's guidance and wisdom. Every battle is an opportunity for your testimony to be written. Over the next few weeks, we will explore how God's wisdom and ways, though unexpected, can lead to your greatest victories. You are being set up for something greater!

WEEK 27: PRAISE GOES FIRST

Read 2 Chronicles 20:17, 22
As you read, underline what God commands them to do.

"You will not need to fight in this battle. Position yourselves, stand still and see the salvation of the Lord, who is with you, O Judah and Jerusalem! Do not fear or be dismayed; tomorrow go out against them, for the Lord is with you.... Now when they began to sing and to praise, the Lord set ambushes against the people of Ammon, Moab, and Mount Seir, who had come against Judah; and they were defeated."

Reflect

Judah was surrounded by hostile enemies. But when Jehoshaphat sought the Lord, God gave him an unexpected and powerful strategy: *Go to the battlefield, stand still, and watch Me fight for you.* The instructions were simple, but they weren't easy. Even though God would fight this battle for them, that doesn't mean they were completely passive. The people of Judah still needed to believe God's word and show up. God's instructions were simple, but obeying them required a lot of faith. Not only did they obey God's command, they also worshipped and praised God as they did so. Confidently standing with God in praise is a powerful battle strategy. It declares to the enemy—and to your own heart—that God is in control, not your circumstances. It shows the enemy that you are relying on God's strength, not your own. It focuses your mind on your all-powerful God instead of your difficulties.

What does it look like to stand firm and praise in the midst of a trial? How might doing so impact your faith?

✻ _____

_____

_____

Give Thanks

List 5 things you are thankful for in this moment.

✻ _____

_____

_____

Pray

Use your prayer time today to praise God! Praise Him for never leaving your side and giving you courage to stand with Him during life's battles.

Take Action

Singing and music are great ways to praise God, but this can occur in all sorts of ways. Brainstorm some unique ways you can praise throughout your daily routine.

✻ _____

_____

_____

WEEK 28:
STRENGTH IN THE UNLIKELY

Read Judges 7:15
As you read, underline what caused Gideon to worship.

"And so it was, when Gideon heard the telling of the dream and its interpretation, that he worshipped. He returned to the camp of Israel, and said, 'Arise, for the Lord has delivered the camp of Midian into your hand.'"

Reflect

For seven long years, Israel suffered at the hands of Midianite invaders who would come and steal their harvest. After hearing the cries of His people, God chose an unlikely man to act as their deliverer: Gideon. Gideon was not a warrior or leader. In fact, he was hiding in fear when God called him to deliver Israel. Overwhelmed by feelings of inadequacy, Gideon questioned that he could lead Israel into battle. But God saw something greater in him. He spoke to Gideon's potential, not his limitations, and strengthened Gideon's resolve and courage with a dream of victory. Like Gideon, we often feel unqualified, unprepared and too small for the tasks God calls us to. We measure ourselves by earthly standards—education, skills, experience, or resources—and conclude we aren't enough. Your feelings of inadequacy or weaknesses don't disqualify you. When you overcome these doubts, you allow yourself to be used by God in mighty ways! He will equip you and give you the strategy you need to overcome every obstacle. All He asks is that you trust boldly and obey Him fully.

Do you feel like an unlikely candidate for God to use? What steps can you take to break through these doubts?

✳ _____
_____
_____

Give Thanks

List 5 things you are thankful for in this moment.

✳ _____
_____
_____

Pray

Ask God to strengthen your resolve today in prayer. Pray for His battle plan to be made clear to you. God may give you a dream or a prophetic word—ask Him to confirm what they mean. Thank Him for the purpose He has put on your life.

Take Action

Read all of Judges 7 to see what happens with Gideon and the Israelites.

✳ _____
_____
_____

WEEK 29: WAITING FOR THE OPPORTUNE MOMENT

Read 2 Samuel 5:23–25
As you read, underline the actions of David.

"Therefore David inquired of the Lord, and He said, 'You shall not go up; circle around behind them, and come upon them in front of the mulberry trees. And it shall be, when you hear the sound of marching in the tops of the mulberry trees, then you shall advance quickly. For then the Lord will go out before you to strike the camp of the Philistines.' And David did so, as the Lord commanded him; and he drove back the Philistines from Geba as far as Gezer."

Reflect

In this passage, David's story is a powerful reminder of humility, dependence, and obedience to God. Though anointed as king, blessed as a warrior, and gifted as a prophet, David never relied on his own strength or past victories. Instead, he remained humble and sought God's counsel. After a recent victory against the Philistines, the same enemy rose to attack again. David could have assumed that he knew what to do and rushed into battle. Instead, he paused, humbled himself, and inquired of God. God instructed David to wait and approach the battle in a specific way. Trusting God's strategy, David obeyed, and the result was another decisive victory! This story teaches us an important truth: Not every battle is the same, and not every victory is won in the same way. When challenges arise, it's easy to rely on our instincts or past experiences. But true success comes when we seek God's guidance. His strategies may not always align with what we expect, but they are always perfect.

How have you experienced God's plan being better than your own? How can you seek God's strategies during challenges in life?

✳ _____

_____

_____

Give Thanks

List 5 things you are thankful for in this moment.

✳ _____

_____

_____

Pray

Use this time to inquire of God like David did. Ask for His strategies and plans to be revealed to you.

Take Action

Meditate on and memorize Isaiah 55:8 this week. Allow this verse to motivate you to seek God's strategies.

✳ _____

_____

_____

WEEK 30: GOD LEADS US TO THE IMPOSSIBLE FIRST

Read Joshua 6:1–2
As you read, underline how Jericho is described.

"Now Jericho was securely shut up because of the children of Israel; none went out, and none came in. And the Lord said to Joshua: 'See! I have given Jericho into your hand, its king, and the mighty men of valor.'"

Reflect

Jericho was a seemingly impossible place to overtake. The city had not one but two walls of defense. The outer wall was 6 feet thick, and the inner was 12 feet thick! Jericho was in Israel's way of claiming the land God had promised them. God led His people to Jericho as their first of many battles. In God's great wisdom, He knew that defeating a seemingly impossible enemy would boost their resolve and faith. While Joshua did not know how to defeat this city, God did. With God's unique plan, the walls fell. Israel was quickly reminded that nothing is impossible with God. What kind of Jerichos are you facing in life? What challenges feel impossible to overcome? Instead of avoiding these obstacles, face them confidently with the knowledge that no challenge is too big for God.

What challenges do you face that feel impossible? How might conquering these with the strategy and strength of the Lord impact your faith?

✳ _____

_____

_____

Give Thanks

List 5 things you are thankful for in this moment.

✳ _____

_____

_____

Pray

Surrender your trials and plans to God today. Trust that He is leading you in the right direction and will help you overcome.

Take Action

When something seems impossible, it can help to remember the promises of God. List a few of God's promises that you can recall when you feel doubtful.

✳ _____

_____

_____

WEEK 31: BREAK FREE FROM SIN

Read Joshua 7:13

As you read, underline the word "sanctify" when it appears.

"Get up, sanctify the people, and say, 'Sanctify yourselves for tomorrow, because thus says the Lord God of Israel: "There is an accursed thing in your midst, O Israel; you cannot stand before your enemies until you take away the accursed thing from among you."'"

Reflect

After miraculously defeating the seemingly impenetrable city of Jericho, Ai was supposed to be an easy conquest. It was only a small city. Yet, when sin and disobedience entered into the hearts of a few, the Israelites suffered a devastating defeat. God didn't abandon His people in their failure but gave them a pathway to restoration. After dealing with the sin in their midst, God instructed Joshua to retake the city of Ai and promised them victory. So complete was this victory that Ai became a permanent city of ruins. Just like the Israelites, our sin can keep us in bondage, limit our potential and prevent us from walking in the fullness of God's power. Sin is a barrier to the victories and breakthroughs God has for us. However, repentance—turning away from sin and seeking God's forgiveness—restores us. Sanctifying yourself involves walking away from habitual sin in your life. When we deal with the sin problem in our lives, we remove barriers to victory and breakthrough!

What sin is limiting you? How can you repent and sanctify yourself before the Lord?

✳ _____
   _____
   _____

Give Thanks

List 5 things you are thankful for in this moment.

✳ _____
   _____
   _____

Pray

Ask the Lord to reveal any unattended sin in your life. He loves you and wants to help you overcome this sin. Seek God's strength and abide in His unconditional love.

Take Action

Write a declaration that sin will not keep you in bondage. Recall this declaration throughout the week as you need it.

✳ _____
   _____
   _____

WEEK 32: GOD IS BIGGER THAN YOUR GIANT

Read 1 Samuel 17:45
As you read, underline how David comes to the Philistine.

"Then David said to the Philistine, 'You come to me with a sword, with a spear, and with a javelin. But I come to you in the name of the Lord of hosts, the God of the armies of Israel, whom you have defied.'"

Reflect

The Philistines sent their fiercest warrior, Goliath, to challenge Israel. If an Israelite could defeat him, the Philistines would surrender the battle. His size and strength paralyzed the entire Israelite army with fear. Everyone, that is, except for David. David wasn't a seasoned warrior. He was young and small and by all appearances, outmatched. But David understood something the others didn't; while Goliath was big, God was infinitely bigger. David's confidence didn't come from his own strength but from his history with God. As a shepherd, he relied on God to help keep his flock safe. Those past victories reminded David that God is always faithful—and this battle would be no different. When David stepped onto the battlefield, he did not rely on his own size or strength. He relied on God's. When you face challenges that feel overwhelming, remember David's story. Victory does not depend on your size, strength, or resources. It depends on your faith in God. The best battle strategy is one that relies completely on God.

How does this passage help put your trials and challenges in perspective?

* _____
  _____

Give Thanks

List 5 things you are thankful for in this moment.

* _____
  _____

Pray

Praise God for His strength and faithfulness. Recount the ways He has helped you overcome in the past. Seek His wisdom as you face opposition.

* _____
  _____

Take Action

Romans 8:31 says, "What then shall we say to these things? If God is for us, who can be against us?" Read and meditate on these words this week.

* _____
  _____

WEEK 33: DESTROYING THE ENEMY'S WORKS

Read 1 John 3:8
As you read, underline why the Son of God was manifested.

"He who sins is of the devil, for the devil has sinned from the beginning. For this purpose the Son of God was manifested, that He might destroy the works of the devil."

Reflect

The Bible makes it clear that we have an enemy—a real adversary who works tirelessly to lead us astray, tempt us into sin, and ultimately try to destroy us. Many of the trials and battles we face are part of the enemy's strategy to pull us away from God and weaken our faith. But here's the incredible truth: We do not face these battles alone. Jesus came to destroy the works of the devil. These "works" are the devil's strategies as he tries to corrupt your heart and mind, make you a slave to sin and doubt God's faithfulness. Sin leads to death, so ultimately, the enemy desires death for all. However, Jesus defeated death on the cross. We walk with the confidence of knowing that the devil and death will not have the final word. In life, there will be temptation, and we might stumble, but we do not have to be enslaved by sin. As you face your battles, remind yourself that Jesus is greater than any enemy that opposes you. We have the power to overcome. In fact, the enemy has already been defeated. Jesus has won the ultimate battle.

What can be your strategy when you face temptation and the works of the enemy?

✳ _____
_____
_____

Give Thanks

List 5 things you are thankful for in this moment.

✳ _____
_____
_____

Pray

Give your thanks to Jesus for defeating the power of sin and conquering death on the cross. Pray that He will give you strength and discernment to recognize the works of the devil and resist.

Take Action

Imagine the devil and his schemes being crushed under the feet of Jesus. Bring this image to mind as you face temptation or hardship this week.

✳ _____
_____
_____

SECTION Seven

FIND HEALING & RESTORATION

Throughout Scripture, we see a powerful and recurring theme: God's heart for restoration and redemption. It is in His very nature to take what is broken and breathe His healing, purpose, and power into it. That includes you! No matter where you've been or what you're facing, God's restoring hand is at work.

As you look ahead, imagine a future fully redeemed by Him! If you're feeling hopeless, God can replenish your hope. If you're feeling weak, He can strengthen you. If your joy has faded, He can restore it! Nothing in your life is too far gone or beyond His reach.

What's truly amazing about God's restoration is that He does not simply replace—He makes things new and better! What He restores becomes a testimony of His glory. Let's explore Scripture to see the redemptive work of God. Allow His promises to stir your faith as you embrace the fullness of life He's created for you.

WEEK 34: REALIGNMENT WITH COVENANT RELATIONSHIPS

Read Genesis 45:25–28
As you read, underline the names Jacob and Israel.

"Then they went up out of Egypt, and came to the land of Canaan to Jacob their father. And they told him, saying, 'Joseph is still alive, and he is governor over all the land of Egypt.' And Jacob's heart stood still, because he did not believe them. But when they told him all the words which Joseph had said to them, and when he saw the carts which Joseph had sent to carry him, the spirit of Jacob their father revived. Then Israel said, 'It is enough. Joseph my son is still alive. I will go and see him before I die.'"

Reflect

Joseph had been sold into slavery by his brothers, but their father believed that Joseph had died. You can imagine his surprise when he learned that his son was not only alive but in a position of power: second in charge over Egypt. Notice that when Jacob decides to reunite with his son, his name changes to Israel. This is significant. Jacob's hope in the covenant blessing of Abraham was renewed. This realignment with God's covenant blessing brought about provision, and they went from a family of about 70 to a nation of 2 million—a nation that still exists today! When we are aligned with our covenant blessing, relationships are restored. These relationships can bring about the provision that comes with that blessing. If you find yourself bearing the burden of a broken relationship, take confidence in the fact that God can restore anything and make it new.

What relationships in your life need restoration? How does this story encourage you in those circumstances?

✳ _____
   _____
   _____

Give Thanks

List 5 things you are thankful for in this moment.

✳ _____
   _____
   _____

Pray

Ask God to restore any relationships that are part of your covenant blessings. Seek His guidance on how you can partner with Him in this process.

Take Action

Recall the relationships you wrote down in the reflection question. How is God calling you to do your part in the restoration process?

✳ _____
   _____
   _____

WEEK 35: GOD HEALS ALL

Read Psalm 103:2–5
As you read, underline the word, "all."

"Bless the Lord, O my soul, And forget not all His benefits: Who forgives all your iniquities, Who heals all your diseases, Who redeems your life from destruction, Who crowns you with lovingkindness and tender mercies, Who satisfies your mouth with good things, So that your youth is renewed like the eagle's."

Reflect

This psalm begins with a powerful shout of praise—a declaration from David's heart, calling on his innermost being to praise God passionately. He reminds himself not to forget all the incredible blessings God has given. David is inspired to praise because God forgives *all* iniquities and heals *all* diseases... not just some of them, but all of them! God is our Healer. There are no limits to God's healing power. He can restore your health today! Sometimes, healing does not come when we expect it, and this can bring frustration, doubt, or pain. When this happens, we feel hope deferred. Even when we do not understand, we can trust God's purposes. Continue to seek Him and have faith that He is the source of all your healing.

Where do you need restored health? Do you believe God can bring healing in this area? Why or why not?

✻ _____

_____

_____

Give Thanks

List 5 things you are thankful for in this moment.

✻ _____

_____

_____

Pray

Pray for God's healing today. Ask Him to restore your health and believe that He CAN do this! Praise Him for how He will bring restoration to your mind and body.

Take Action

Throughout the week, make an effort to meditate on these verses, memorizing them.

✻ _____

_____

_____

WEEK 36: GOD'S RESTITUTION

Read Job 42:10–11
As you read, underline who restored Job's losses.

"And the Lord restored Job's losses when he prayed for his friends. Indeed the Lord gave Job twice as much as he had before. Then all his brothers, all his sisters, and all those who had been his acquaintances before, came to him and ate food with him in his house; and they consoled him and comforted him for all the adversity that the Lord had brought upon him. Each one gave him a piece of silver and each a ring of gold."

Reflect

Job had lost pretty much everything but his life—his family, his livelihood, and even his health. He endured great suffering and loss. Through his story, we learn that God is not blind to our pain and can bring restoration to our lives—even if we have lost everything. You probably have not experienced the level of hardship that Job did, but you have likely lost something in your life—a job, an opportunity, a relationship. Restoration does not mean simply replacing what is lost. It means making something new and better than before. We learn in Matthew that God is faithful to provide for His children. Knowing God's power of restoration and His promise to provide can bring us hope when we feel all is lost. It can bring us peace during financial hardship. We can have hope that something better is on the horizon!

What steps can you take to trust more in God's provision and restoration?

✱ _____

_____

_____

Give Thanks

List 5 things you are thankful for in this moment.

✱ _____

_____

_____

Pray

Job was honest with God. He never hid his confusion or frustration. You too can be authentic with your Heavenly Father. But even as you express your concerns, remember to infuse your prayer with trust and worship.

Take Action

Our community makes a big difference in our faith. Some of Job's friends had bad advice, others had good, godly advice. Who can you trust to encourage you when you experience loss? Reach out to them this week!

✱ _____

_____

_____

WEEK 37: GOD RESTORES YOUR REST

Read Psalm 23:1–3
As you read, underline what the Lord does for the psalmist (and for you).

"The Lord is my shepherd; I shall not want. He makes me to lie down in green pastures; He leads me beside the still waters. He restores my soul; He leads me in the paths of righteousness For His name's sake."

Reflect

Rest might feel like a luxury in today's fast-paced world. Maybe it even feels lazy or indulgent. Nothing could be further from the truth. Rest is vitally important to your physical, emotional, and spiritual health. From the very beginning, God set a standard for us. After creating the earth for six days, God rested from work on the seventh day. He gave us the gift of sabbath: a day devoted to rest and abiding in the Lord. We live in a world that prioritizes busyness and hustle. While there is nothing wrong with hard work, there is also value in finding rest. Rest is not about doing nothing; it's about creating space for God to restore and refresh you. If deep, meaningful rest feels impossible, God can bring restoration in this area. This psalm paints a beautiful picture of the kind of rest only God can provide. When we pause and embrace stillness, we are able to reconnect with our Savior on a deeper level. It's a reminder that God is the ultimate provider and sustainer, and rest is an act of trust, releasing control back to Him. In this chaotic world, God is inviting you to rest. Embrace this beautiful gift starting today!

What does intentional rest for your soul look like? What activities does this involve or not involve?

* _____
 _____
 _____

Give Thanks

List 5 things you are thankful for in this moment.

* _____
 _____
 _____

Pray

Ask God to help you rest. Be honest with Him about how you struggle with this and seek His guidance. Give Him praise for restoring your soul with the gift of rest.

Take Action

Make a plan to sabbath one day this week. It can be any day, and it involves relying on God's restoration as you step away from stressful work and busyness. If this feels daunting, you can start with half a day.

* _____
 _____
 _____

WEEK 38: THE JOY OF THE LORD

Read Psalm 30:5
As you read, underline what comes in the morning.

"Weeping may endure for a night, But joy comes in the morning."

Reflect

While we are never promised a life free from struggles or pain, we are promised something far greater: joy. The Bible speaks of joy often! Unlike happiness that comes and goes depending on our circumstances, joy is lasting. Happiness can be fleeting, but joy runs deep. If you are facing seasons of grief, disappointment, or loss, this verse gives you hope. The night is never permanent, and joy will come in the morning. It will help you endure times of despair. Nehemiah 8:10 says that the joy of the Lord is our strength! If you feel like this joy is lost, know that God can restore your joy. As He opens your eyes to His presence and redemption, the joy will come. You can count on it!

How has the joy of the Lord helped you in times of difficulty?

✱ _____
_____
_____

Give Thanks

List 5 things you are thankful for in this moment.

✽ _____

_____

_____

Pray

In your prayer, ask for the joy of God to fill you and give you strength. Offer Him your thanks for making this joy available to you today.

Take Action

How can you remind yourself of God's joy throughout your week, especially during difficult moments?

✽ _____

_____

_____

WEEK 39: RENEWING STRENGTH

Read Isaiah 40:29–31
As you read, underline the word "strength" when it appears.

"He gives power to the weak, And to those who have no might He increases strength. Even the youths shall faint and be weary, And the young men shall utterly fall, But those who wait on the Lord Shall renew their strength; They shall mount up with wings like eagles, They shall run and not be weary, They shall walk and not faint."

Reflect

Isaiah spent the first 28 verses telling us all about the power and glory of God. Then in verse 29, we learn something amazing: God offers us that very same power. It's a humbling truth—this mighty strength is available to us! Yet to receive it, we cannot rely on our own strength. For those who humble themselves and wait on the Lord, strength beyond measure is promised to them. Waiting on the Lord doesn't mean we passively sit around and do nothing. It is an active waiting—a time of seeking, trusting, and relying on God's power to sustain and renew us. It's about drawing near to Him and allowing His strength to become ours. And the result? A renewed endurance that allows us to rise above our challenges. The word "weary" in these verses speaks to the exhaustion that comes from life's struggles. We all face moments when life feels overwhelming, but here's the amazing truth—God promises to give us the strength to soar above those challenges. With His power, we can keep moving forward, stronger and more determined than ever, for His glory!

What could change in your life if you received this restoration of strength?

* _____
  _____
  _____

Give Thanks

List 5 things you are thankful for in this moment.

* _____
  _____
  _____

Pray

Praise God for the gift of His power and strength! Ask that He helps you rely on His strength rather than your own.

Take Action

How can you wait on God this week?

* _____
  _____
  _____

WEEK 40: FILLED TO THE BRIM WITH HOPE

Read Romans 15:13
As you read, underline the words "abound in hope" when it appears.

"Now may the God of hope fill you with all joy and peace in believing, that you may abound in hope by the power of the Holy Spirit."

Reflect

The God of hope—what a powerful and beautiful title for our Lord! It reminds us not only *where* hope comes from but *who* generously pours it into our lives. As Christians, our lives are meant to radiate hope and a confident expectation rooted in Christ's return and the eternal glory we will share with Him. Unlike the world around us, we don't anchor our trust in unstable foundations like politics, finances, or the actions of flawed people. Our hope is in the unchanging, all-powerful God. Even when life feels overwhelming and trials press in from every side, we are never without hope! Paul's prayer in Romans is that God would fill us with so much hope that it overflows. And here's the best part: All that's required from us is to believe. Does your heart feel weary today? Has life drained some of your hope? God's supply of hope is endless. Seek Him and He will restore not just your hope, but also your joy and peace.

What does it look like to abound in hope? How would being full of hope impact your day-to-day life?

✳ _____

_____

_____

Give Thanks

List 5 things you are thankful for in this moment.

✳ _____

_____

_____

Pray

Use Paul's words in this verse to inspire your prayer today. Pray for the God of hope to fill you up!

Take Action

When your hope feels a little depleted this week, what can you do to seek God's restoration?

✳ _____

_____

_____

WEEK 41: SHALOM SHALOM

Read Isaiah 26:3
As you read, underline what the author says God will do.

"You will keep him in perfect peace, Whose mind is stayed on You, Because he trusts in You."

Reflect

Perfect peace—it sounds almost too good to be true in a world filled with chaos, uncertainty and distractions. Yet this is exactly what God promises. It is not a fleeting or shallow peace, but a deep, unwavering calm that anchors your soul, no matter what storms rage around you. In this verse, Isaiah says that not only does God give us peace, He keeps us in it. And this isn't just any peace, it is perfect peace. This phrase in Hebrew is *Shalom Shalom*. Using the word twice signifies intensity. The key to this peace lies in where our minds are focused. When our thoughts are steadfast—fixed on God's goodness, His promises, and His unchanging character—peace follows. This does not mean ignoring or denying life's challenges, but rather choosing to trust that God is bigger than any obstacle. He is faithful to carry us through. We might experience peace in places or things, but it will never be the *perfect* peace of God. Fortunately, God's peace is always available to us. If you are lacking peace today, it can be restored! Turn your mind to the Lord and trust in His promises.

How does this promise from God motivate and encourage you today?

* _____
  _____
  _____

Give Thanks

List 5 things you are thankful for in this moment.

* _____
  _____
  _____

Pray

Give God glory for His perfect peace available to you! Thank Him for never breaking His promises and seek His help as you keep your thoughts focused on Him.

Take Action

What steps can you take to keep your mind on God this week?

* _____
  _____
  _____

WEEK 42: REDEEMING TIME

Read Ephesians 5:15–16
As you read, underline what Paul says to redeem.

"See then that you walk circumspectly, not as fools but as wise, redeeming the time, because the days are evil."

Reflect

In this passage, Paul offers a practical and powerful wisdom for living out our faith each day. He calls us to walk circumspectly—to live carefully, intentionally, and with purpose. Why? Because time is precious. Distractions, worries, sin, and worldly priorities can pull us off course, leaving us unfulfilled, unproductive, and short of what God has purposed for us. But here's the good news: Scripture says that we can redeem lost time. The word "redeem" means to buy back. It implies a sacrifice on our part—it costs us. The word "time" is the Greek word *kairos*, which means opportune moment or opportunity. This means that God is able to help us recover lost opportunities. By aligning our life with His will and seeking His kingdom first, we take back what might otherwise be lost. When we are intentional with our days, devoting them to the Lord and our God given purpose, we find our lives become more fulfilling and joyful.

How can you be more intentional and careful with your time?

✽ _____
_____
_____

Give Thanks

List 5 things you are thankful for in this moment.

✽ _____
_____
_____

Pray

Ask God to help you walk wisely. Pray for His guidance and conviction as you go about your day.

Take Action

What things distract you from using your time wisely? Brainstorm ways you can set up boundaries around those distractions this week.

✽ _____
_____
_____

WEEK 43: PREPARE TO CROSS OVER

Read Joshua 3:5–6
As you read, underline the three things Joshua says to do.

"And Joshua said to the people, 'Sanctify yourselves, for tomorrow the Lord will do wonders among you.' Then Joshua spoke to the priests, saying, 'Take up the ark of the covenant and cross over before the people.'"

Reflect

These verses take place right before the Israelites go and claim the Promised Land. This is a pivotal moment for them. They knew that battles lay ahead, yet instead of focusing on military strategies, they chose to sanctify themselves. This isn't just a physical preparation—they cleansed themselves spiritually, getting right with God. Sanctification focused their minds on God and set them apart from those who inhabited the land. If we desire spiritual breakthrough, we must be willing to be set apart from the world around us. The Holy Spirit sanctifies us in life, but this process also involves effort on our end. While salvation is a gift we receive through grace, living a life that reflects God's glory requires intentional effort on our part. The Israelites had to cross over the Jordan River. We need to cross over our own personal Jordan into a life defined by God's glory and purposes.

Why is it important to prepare your heart for God's wonders in your life?

* _____
  _____
  _____

Give Thanks

List 5 things you are thankful for in this moment.

* _____
  _____
  _____

Pray

Praise God for making you righteous through the blood of Jesus. Ask for His help as you seek to sanctify yourself and walk in a manner worthy of your calling.

Take Action

What can you do this week to sanctify and set yourself apart from the world?

* _____
  _____
  _____

SECTION Eight

DEVELOP AN EXPECTATION OF THE FUTURE

You have come such a long way in this devotional, and what a journey it has been. Along the way, you have opened your heart to God's truth and love, allowing Him to realign your life with His purposes and set you free from the things that have held you back in the past. You've trusted Him to deliver you from fear and doubt. You've allowed yourself to believe again in the promises He's spoken over your life. You have armed yourself with His battle strategies and found the healing and restoration your soul longed for!

So what's next? As you step into the final section of this devotional, it's time to look forward with faith. You may not know every detail of God's plan, but you can trust Him completely to hold your future secure. Because of God, your path ahead is filled with victory, purpose, and the fulfillment of His promises.

It's easy to get caught up in the past, but now is the time to break free and embrace a new perspective. Choose to look forward with hope and allow faith to guide you as you step into the incredible things God has prepared. Your best days are ahead. The God who brought you this far will lead you to His abundant future!

WEEK 44: NOTHING IS IMPOSSIBLE FOR GOD

Read Luke 18:27
As you read, underline the words "impossible" and "possible."

"But He said, 'The things which are impossible with men are possible with God.'"

Reflect

This verse is a reminder of God's limitless power and faithfulness. In life, we often face challenges that seem insurmountable—relationships that feel broken beyond repair, dreams that seem out of reach, or circumstances that appear hopeless. But this verse calls us to shift our perspective. What may seem impossible is entirely possible for God. The Bible is full of stories about God's power, might, knowledge, and miracle-working abilities. When you feel overwhelmed, remember that God is not bound by human limitations. He makes a way where there is none, turning setbacks into opportunities and bringing life to what seems lost. Bring your impossible situations to God. Believe that He is working behind the scenes in ways you cannot see yet. With God, nothing is too hard, too far gone, or too late.

How might your life change if you embraced the truth that nothing is impossible for God?

✱ _____

_____

_____

Give Thanks

List 5 things you are thankful for in this moment.

✱ _____

_____

_____

Pray

In your prayer today, ask God to show you what's possible in your life through Him! Praise Him for all He has done and will do in the future!

Take Action

What feels impossible in life right now? How can you surrender this to the Lord this week?

✱ _____

_____

_____

WEEK 45: BLESSED WITH EVERY SPIRITUAL BLESSING

Read Ephesians 1:3
As you read, underline the words "blessed" and "blessings."

"Blessed be the God and Father of our Lord Jesus Christ, who has blessed us with every spiritual blessing in the heavenly places in Christ."

Reflect

As you look ahead to your future, take heart—you are not walking this journey empty-handed. God has already equipped you with *every spiritual blessing in Christ!* These blessings go far beyond the physical and temporal; they are eternal treasures rooted in God's heavenly purposes. While physical gifts are wonderful and can bring joy, they pale in comparison to the spiritual inheritance that never fades. Notice that the word "blessed" in this verse is in the past tense. That means these blessings are not something we're waiting for; they've already been poured out on us through Jesus! They are secure, complete, and eternal—given freely by God's grace and can only be experienced through a relationship with Him. In this passage, Paul invites us to embrace and rejoice in our spiritual riches. When you wake up each day, no matter what your circumstances look like, you can declare with confidence that you are spiritually rich in Christ. These blessings include salvation, our adoption as His children, grace, redemption, forgiveness, wisdom, the indwelling of the Holy Spirit, and the promise of eternal life—gifts that empower you to live boldly for His glory. Let this truth shape how you see your future. The God who has blessed you abundantly in the past is the same God who walks with you now and holds your tomorrow.

How does this passage encourage you and give you confidence for your future?

✽ _____

_____

Give Thanks

List 5 things you are thankful for in this moment.

✽ _____

_____

Pray

Offer your worship and thanks to God for His generosity. Write your prayer in the space provided.

✽ _____

_____

Take Action

Paul goes on to describe these blessings even more! This week, read the entire chapter of Ephesians 1.

✽ _____

_____

WEEK 46: ABOVE ALL THAT YOU CAN ASK OR THINK

Read Ephesians 3:20–21
As you read, underline what God is able to do.

"Now to Him who is able to do exceedingly abundantly above all that we ask or think, according to the power that works in us, to Him be glory in the church by Christ Jesus to all generations, forever and ever. Amen."

Reflect

This passage is a breathtaking reminder of the limitless power of God at work in our lives. It declares that God is able to do exceedingly abundantly. This isn't just a promise of meeting our expectations—it's a declaration that His plans far exceed anything we can dream of. Whatever you imagined, God not only can accomplish that but so much more. He works through His power that is alive in us, shaping our lives, our circumstances, and even our hearts in ways that are beyond human comprehension. Even though the context in Ephesians is for Christ to dwell in you fully, His goodness and power also work in all areas of your lives! There is no area of your life where God cannot create abundance and transformation! This verse is in the present tense. God is, *right now*, able to do immeasurably more and bring you to your full potential.

How does this verse impact the way you seek God and what you ask of Him?

* _____
  _____
  _____

Give Thanks

List 5 things you are thankful for in this moment.

* _____
  _____
  _____

Pray

Ask for God to fill you with the fullness of Christ! Worship the Lord who can do far more than anything you ever imagined.

Take Action

This truth is followed by a call to worship—to God be the glory! How can you give God glory this week?

* _____
  _____
  _____

WEEK 47:
PRESS TOWARD THE GOAL

Read Philippians 3:12–14
As you read, underline the four things Paul says he does.

"Not that I have already attained, or am already perfected; but I press on, that I may lay hold of that for which Christ Jesus has also laid hold of me. Brethren, I do not count myself to have apprehended; but one thing I do, forgetting those things which are behind and reaching forward to those things which are ahead, I press toward the goal for the prize of the upward call of God in Christ Jesus."

Reflect

Have you ever felt stuck in the past—whether in regret, failure, or even moments of success? Paul's words are a rallying cry to break free and press forward. Paul's language here is alive with purpose: *press on, lay hold of*. These are not passive actions; they are bold, determined pursuits. To *press on* means to run with focus and intention, and to *lay hold of* implies grabbing tightly, refusing to let go. Paul reminds us that our relationship with God requires focus, passion, and an unwavering commitment to keep moving forward. He is encouraging us to never settle when it comes to our relationship with God. Why is that? For the sake of the ultimate prize: knowing Christ fully and becoming more like Him. This isn't about striving in our own strength but relying on God's grace as we move forward with His plan in our lives. So, don't settle. Press on with everything you've got, fixing your eyes on the goal. Keep moving forward—one step, one moment, one act of faith at a time.

What does it look like to eagerly pursue and move energetically toward the call of God in your own life?

✳ _____

_____

_____

Give Thanks

List 5 things you are thankful for in this moment.

✳ _____

_____

_____

Pray

You can be honest in your prayers, bringing your authentic self. Express to God what is tripping you up on your spiritual walk. Ask that He helps you overcome and press on.

Take Action

What can you do to help you press on toward the goal of Christ on days when you feel like giving up?

✳ _____

_____

_____

WEEK 48: STRENGTH FOR EVERY SEASON

Read Philippians 4:13
As you read, underline what Christ does for Paul (and for you).

"I can do all things through Christ who strengthens me."

Reflect

Paul had just described how he knew life's struggles intimately. He had times of abundance and comfort, but he also faced hardship and hunger. Yet he boldly declared that he's learned the secret of being content in *any and every situation*. The secret? He discovered where true strength lies—not in himself, his abilities or his possessions, but in God. We too will go through different seasons and circumstances, but we can thrive and find contentment in all of them because of God's strength in us. Paul understood that God never calls without equipping. The same is true for you. Whatever God calls you to do, He will equip you for it. You are never on your own. God is always with you, strengthening you. You can overcome every obstacle, accomplish every task, and endure every hardship. All because of His power working within you. No matter what the future holds, you can do all things through Christ!

How might memorizing this verse impact the way you face challenges in life?

✻ _____

_____

Give Thanks

List 5 things you are thankful for in this moment.

✻ _____

_____

Pray

What season of life are you in right now? Talk about it with God. Ask that He continues to strengthen you to be faithful.

✻ _____

_____

Take Action

List the ways God has given you strength in life. On days when you feel overwhelmed or weak, recall this list and remind yourself of God's faithfulness.

✻ _____

_____

WEEK 49: EMPOWERED FOR GREATER WORKS

Read John 14:12–14
As you read, underline what those who believe in Jesus will do.

"Most assuredly, I say to you, he who believes in Me, the works that I do he will do also; and greater works than these he will do, because I go to My Father. And whatever you ask in My name, that I will do, that the Father may be glorified in the Son. If you ask anything in My name, I will do it."

Reflect

This is an incredibly empowering passage. Jesus, in His infinite wisdom, saw great things in the future of those who believe in Him—that includes you! It might sound unbelievable, but Jesus declared that your works could surpass His own. Let's unpack this. Jesus walked the earth in a limited geographic area, remaining in Palestine for His entire ministry. However, He had a much bigger plan—that His disciples and you will carry His message to the furthest corners of the world, reaching people across all nations, cultures and generations. You are part of this extraordinary mission! As followers of Jesus, you are called to break barriers and shine His light wherever you go. Take a moment to reflect on your expectations for the future. How do you expect to impact the world around you? Embrace Jesus' words in this passage and dream big! As we read in one of the previous passages, what He has planned for you is far more than what you can ask or imagine.

Verse 13 shows us that prayer plays a vital role in living out this call. What does your prayer life look like? How do you want to grow in prayer? Write down some steps you can take to deepen your connection with God through prayer.

✽ _____

_____

_____

Give Thanks

List 5 things you are thankful for in this moment.

✽ _____

_____

_____

Pray

Praying in Jesus' name means to pray in alignment with His will. In your prayer today, ask God to show what good works He has planned for you. Ask for the strength to walk in His purposes.

Take Action

Doing the great things Jesus has planned for you requires obedience! How can you be obedient to what Jesus is calling you to this week?

✽ _____

_____

_____

WEEK 50: FAITH THAT SEES

Read Hebrews 11:1
As you read, underline the word faith.

"Now faith is the substance of things hoped for, the evidence of things not seen. For by it the elders obtained a good testimony."

Reflect

Faith isn't just something we hold in our hearts or think about in our minds—it's meant to shape the way we live, moment by moment. It is not an emotion or wishful thinking—it has substance and evidence. The word "substance" in this verse literally refers to a foundation that something is built on. It represents something solid and strong, and it refers to our unshakable confidence in God! Faith gives us confidence to step out when the path seems unclear and to trust when our hearts are weighed down by unanswered prayers. Faith is not just blind optimism; it is also *evidence*. In the rest of the chapter, we see the evidence of faith in people's lives as they trust God. Our faith is rooted in the character of God, who is unchanging and never fails. When life is uncertain or overwhelming, this verse calls us to shift our focus from what we see to the One we trust. So even though some of God's promises have yet to happen, we can walk into the future with a confident expectation that they will come to be, even if we can't see it yet.

How are you currently activating your faith in the things you cannot see?

✳ _____
_____

Give Thanks

List 5 things you are thankful for in this moment.

✳ _____
_____

Pray

Praise God for His promises and ask Him to strengthen your faith where it might waver. You can write your prayer in the space provided.

✳ _____
_____

Take Action

What steps can you take this week to strengthen your faith in areas where it feels weak or uncertain?

✳ _____
_____

WEEK 51: LEAN NOT ON YOUR OWN UNDERSTANDING

Read Proverbs 3:5–6

As you read, underline how the author says to trust the Lord.

"Trust in the Lord with all your heart, And lean not on your own understanding; In all your ways acknowledge Him, And He shall direct your paths."

Reflect

When it comes to our future, trusting anyone—even God—can feel risky. We're often tempted to rely on ourselves. But these two verses reveal a radically different way to live—one of *complete dependence* on God. Trusting God is an all or nothing invitation. The author tells us to trust the Lord with *all our heart.* This kind of trust is a full surrender that brings about a powerful transformation. When we let go of our need to control every outcome and choose instead to lean on God, we find a peace that does not depend on circumstances. When we stop leaning on our own limited understanding and start acknowledging God in every way, He will direct our paths. It's simple, yet life-changing. Trust Him. Acknowledge Him. Follow His lead. When we do so, we unlock a future full of confidence and purpose.

Do you ever find yourself only partially trusting God, depending on Him for some things but not others? What could change in life if you fully surrendered and trusted God with your *whole* heart?

* _____
  _____
  _____

Give Thanks

List 5 things you are thankful for in this moment.

* _____
  _____
  _____

Pray

If you struggle to trust God with all your heart, talk to Him about this and seek His help. He understands your struggles and loves you no matter what!

Take Action

To acknowledge God means to know Him, to seek His presence, and abide in His love. How can you acknowledge Him this week?

* _____
  _____
  _____

WEEK 52: FROM FEAR TO CONFIDENCE!

Read Deuteronomy 31:6
As you read, underline what the Lord does.

"Be strong and of good courage, do not fear nor be afraid of them; for the Lord your God, He is the One who goes with you. He will not leave you nor forsake you."

Reflect

These are Moses' last words to Israel before his death. Their time of wandering in the desert had come to an end and they were about to take the Promised Land. While they knew God had promised this land, they did not know what waited for them on the other side—what battles they would have to face or obstacles to cross. Looking to the future can be scary. There are so many unknowns and what ifs. But it is possible to face the uncertainties of life with courage, peace, and confidence. Why? Because God promises to be with you. He will never leave your side. When the Creator of the universe is strengthening you and fighting for you, there is nothing you cannot overcome.

What situations in your life right now require strength and courage? How can you apply Moses' words to those circumstances?

✳ _____

_____

_____

Give Thanks

List 5 things you are thankful for in this moment.

✳ _____

_____

_____

Pray

In your prayer today, ask God to remind you of His presence with you. Praise Him for the courage and confidence you can have in Him!

Take Action

What are some practical ways you can remind yourself of God's presence this week when you feel afraid or anxious?

✳ _____

_____

_____

CONCLUSION

Your journey begins: Step boldly into God's promise!

We've reached the end of our 52 weeks together, but this is far from the end of your story. This is the beginning of a powerful new chapter in your walk with God. Over the past year, you've shown up with faith, courage, and determination. You've dived deep into God's word, letting it renew your mind and transform your heart. You've released the weight of the past, surrendered your fears, and embraced your inheritance in Christ.

As you step forward into the future, know this: God is with you every step of the way. His presence surrounds you, His strength sustains you, and His love never fails.

Remember Paul's words in Romans, 8:31, "What then shall we say to these things? If God is for us, who can be against us?" With God on your side, no challenge is too great, no obstacle too daunting. You can face the future with unshakable confidence, leaning on His strength, wisdom, and perfect plan for your life.

Your best days are ahead, and the journey God has prepared for you is greater than you can imagine. The best is yet to come—step into it with faith and boldness!

REFERENCES

Holy Bible. (1982). The New King James Version. Thomas Nelson.

Made in the USA
Columbia, SC
02 July 2025